Tax-Smart Exit Strategies:

Financial Gravity's Quick Guide to *Dis*-Inviting the IRS From Your Next Taxable Event

Edward A. Lyon, JD

Tax-Smart Exit Strategies:
Financial Gravity's Quick Guide to *Dis*-Inviting The IRS From Your Next Taxable Event

Copyright © 2019 by Financial Gravity Companies

All rights reserved. No part of this book may be reproduced or transmitted in any form or by any means without written permission from the author.

Contents

1. Introduction 1
2. How Capital Gains Work 7
3. Installment Sales 13
   Structured Sales 18
   "Installment Sale Coupled With Monetizing Loan" 19
   Strategies For Your Business 23
   Employee Stock Ownership Plan 24
   Section 1202 Stock 26
4. Strategies for Real Estate 29
   Section 121 Exclusion 30
   Section 1031 Exchanges 33
5. Charitable Strategies 39
   Charitable Remainder Trust 40
   Pooled Income Fund 47
6. Strategies For Your Portfolio 53
   Strategies for Mutual Funds 53
   Tax Loss Harvesting 59
   Tax-Engineered Products 60
8. After-Sale Offsets 63
   Charitable Gifts 64
   Oil & Gas 67
9. Qualified Opportunity Zones 69
   Tax Deferral 70
   Qualified Opportunity Fund 71

1. Introduction

> "If you are truly serious about preparing your child for the future, don't teach him how to subtract, teach him how to deduct."
>
> **Fran Lebowitz**

Congratulations! You've made a killing! A fortune! Or at least a *profit*! And now you're ready to sell, to cash in on those hard-earned gains.

Maybe you'll host a celebratory dinner or throw a party to celebrate your success. You'll invite your spouse, your children, and your friends. You'll find a caterer and hire servers to take care of them while they congratulate you on your good fortune.

But look over in the other direction. Who's that getting out of their car . . . ? Could it be . . . ? Wait a minute . . . you didn't invite those guys! What's the IRS doing, crashing your party?!?!

It's sad but true. It doesn't matter how you made your killing. The IRS wants a slice of the pie. (And why shouldn't they? Pie is delicious.)

Some tax professionals will tell you to just suck it up and pay. "You made the money," they'll reason with you. "Now it's time pay up." They'll quote Benjamin Franklin: "Nothing is certain in life but death and taxes," and tell you to be glad you're just trying to avoid taxes, and not death. They'll remind you that taxes on capital gains are capped at special, lower rates (but maybe forget to remind you about the new net investment income tax). It's no skin off *their* back. Also, it's not their *money*.

Here at Financial Gravity, we don't think that way. We're glad to see you enjoy a nice gain. (Sometimes we'll even help you make it.) We understand that Uncle Sam wants his share, and we appreciate that he's willing to take a slightly skinnier slice when it's long-term capital gains. But we also understand that there are lots of ways to avoid paying that slice – to shrink it, defer it, and sometimes even eliminate it entirely.

Let's take a 30,000-foot look at how the tax code works so we can explain how we're different. You've heard of the Infinite Monkey Theorem, right? Give an infinite number of monkeys an infinite number of typewriters, and sooner or later, one of them will bang out the complete works of William Shakespeare.

Do you know what sort of gibberish they're banging out when they're not banging out Shakespeare? The tax code, of course. There's a reason former President Jimmy Carter once called it "a disgrace to the human race."

So here's a quick analogy to make some sense out of the much-maligned code. Think of the entire thing – all 2,600+ pages of it – as a series of red lights and green lights. The red lights are where you have to stop and pay tax; the green lights are where you don't.

> ### The Tax Code, Decoded
>
> § 1: Tax Imposed
>
>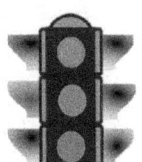
>
> (a) MARRIED INDIVIDUALS FILING JOINT RETURNS AND SURVIVING SPOUSES There is hereby imposed on the taxable income of—
>
> (1) every married individual (as defined in section 7703) who makes a single return jointly with his spouse under section 6013, and
>
> (2) every surviving spouse (as defined in section 2(a)),
>
> a tax determined in accordance with [the tax table]

Look at the very front of the Code, Section 1(a): Tax Imposed.

> *"There is hereby imposed on the taxable income of every married individual (as defined in section 7703) who makes a single return jointly with his spouse under section 6013, and every surviving spouse – as defined in section 2(a) – a tax determined in accordance with [the tax table]."*

It's pretty straightforward. Joint filers owe tax, and here's how much. That's a red light. Stop and pay tax. Section 1(b), 1(c), and 1(d) go on to lay out the rates for single filers, heads of households, and separate filers.

Section 1401 imposes the self-employment tax and sets the rate. That's another red light.

Section 1411 imposes the net investment income tax on investment income, including capital gains, for filers with adjusted gross income (AGI) over $200,000 (single filers) or $250,000 (joint filers). That's another red light.

> ### The Tax Code, Decoded
>
>
>
> **§ 101: Certain Death Benefits**
>
> (a) P<small>ROCEEDS OF LIFE INSURANCE CONTRACTS PAYABLE BY REASON OF DEATH</small>
>
> (1) G<small>ENERAL RULE</small>
>
> Except as otherwise provided in paragraph (2), subsection (d), subsection (f), and subsection (j), gross income does not include amounts received (whether in a single sum or otherwise) under a life insurance contract, if such amounts are paid by reason of the death of the insured.

But the code includes more than just *red* lights. There are green lights, too.

- Code Section 101, for example, which says that life insurance death benefits are generally nontaxable. When you see the words "gross income does not include," you're seeing a green light.

- Code Section 105(b) provides that "gross income does not include" employer-provided health benefits.

- Code Section 162 says "there shall be allowed as a deduction," ordinary and necessary business expenses. When you see the words "there shall be allowed as a deduction," you're seeing a green light.

- Code Section 170 says "there shall be allowed as a deduction," any charitable contribution (verified under "regulations prescribed by the Secretary.")

- Code Section 179 says that any qualifying business property the taxpayer chooses not to expense "shall be allowed as a deduction."

Oh, and just to make things even more fun, don't forget that you can turn right on a red light! What's the tax equivalent? Let's say you're single, age 40, you net $200,000 from your business, and you want to stuff $30,000 into a Roth IRA. You can't do that, of course. Your AGI is well above the limit for contributing (a red light), and even if it's not, contributions are limited to $5,500 per year (another red light). But . . . you *can* put $30,000 into a Simplified Employee Pension (SEP) and immediately convert *that* to a Roth. That strategy, also known as a "backdoor Roth," lets you turn right on red!

Here's what sets Financial Gravity apart from anyone else you've worked with. Most tax professionals focus their eyes on the red lights. And that's important! Blowing through the red lights is how you get in trouble, so they want to keep you out of trouble. But the tax code actually has more green lights than red lights. And if all you pay attention to is the reds, you miss all those opportunities to save with the green!"

So that's what this book is about: finding the green lights (and places where you can turn right on red) that let you "go" without paying taxes (or paying less, or paying later), when it comes to your capital gains.

Edward A. Lyon, JD CTM

2. How Capital Gains Work

> "The first nine pages of the Internal Revenue Code define income; the remaining 1,100 pages spin the web of exceptions and preferences."
>
> **Sen. Warren Magnuson**

Buy low. Sell high. Pay tax on the difference.

That's the basic concept, in nine words. And if that's all there was, this wouldn't be much of a book.

Of course, when it comes to taxes, it's never that easy. As the Genie says in Disney's *Aladdin*, there are always "a few, uh, provisos, ah, a couple of quid pro quo." And as Senator Warren Magnuson so accurately said, "the first nine pages of the Internal Revenue Code define income; the remaining 1,100 pages spin the web of exceptions and preferences. (I'm not sure when Magnuson actually said that, but I can safely report he died in 1989 – meaning Congress has added one significant red light and several thousand pages of green lights since then!)

With that in mind, let's unpack those nine words and lay down a foundation for understanding the rest of the book:

1. **Buy Low.** The first question you have to answer in order to calculate tax on gain is the cost you pay for it. Technically, this can include "original basis," "adjusted basis," and "recomputed basis." However, to keep your head from spinning, we'll just call it "basis." Basis includes what you pay for an asset, including any commissions, fees, or other expenses. It includes cash out of your own pocket, as well as anything you borrow to pay for the asset. It also includes additions, like improvements or renovations to a house, and subtractions, like depreciation and amortization of intangible assets. The IRS publishes an entire 13-page guide, in the usual three columns and tiny print, to walk you through this process.

2. **Sell High.** The next question involves how much you take away from the sale. This process starts with your gross sale price, then subtracts any commissions or other expenses you pay to sell your property. Your sale price includes anything used to pay off debt at closing. (Plenty of unhappy sellers have found themselves bringing cash to a closing, and *still* walking away with a tax bill!)

3. **Pay Tax on the Difference.** Subtract adjusted basis from adjusted sales price, and *voila*, you have your taxable gain!

It would be easy if that was all you had to do. So now it's time for some bad news and some good news. The bad news is, there can be different types of taxes for different types of gains. The good news is, those differences create opportunities to pay less! So now let's look at those differences.

- Short-term gains are gains from sale of property you've held for up to one year. Under current law, those are taxed as ordinary income.

- Long-term gains are gains from the sale of property you've held for longer than a year. These are generally taxed at special, preferential rates.

Long-Term Capital Gains (2019)

Tax Rate	Single	Joint
0%	$ 0 – 39,375	$ 0 – 78,750
15%	$ 39,376 – 434,550	$ 78,751 – 488,850
20%	$ 434,551+	$ 488,851+

If you've taken depreciation deductions on the property you're selling, you may have to "recapture" some or all of it on the sale. Gains from recapturing depreciation on personal property are taxed as ordinary income (because you deducted those amounts as ordinary income). Gains from recapturing depreciation on real estate are classified as "unrecaptured Section 1250 gain" and taxed at no higher than 25%.

Finally, some assets get special treatment that can help you or hurt you when it comes time to sell:

- Gains from the sale of collectibles (works of art, rugs, antiques, precious metals such as gold, silver, and platinum bullion, gems, stamps, coins, alcoholic beverages, and certain other tangible properties) are taxed at a special 28% rate, even if you've held them long enough to otherwise qualify for the top 20% rate.

- Gains from the sale of your primary residence are nontaxable, up to $250,000 for single filers and $500,000 for joint filers, if you've owned it and occupied it as your primary residence for two out of the last five years. (You can exclude a pro-rata portion of the gain if you fail to meet the two-year requirement due to "unforeseen circumstances" like a job transfer or health conditions.)

When it comes time to file your return, you'll gather information from all sorts of sources. Typically, these include Form 1099-DIV (for mutual fund capital gain distributions), Form 1099-B (for sales from stock and brokerage accounts), and Form K1 (from partnerships or S corporations you own that sold assets during the year). If you sold real estate or business assets that you owned in your own name, you'll report those gains on Form 4797. You'll aggregate all those gains on Schedule D, and your tax preparer will calculate how much you owe on short-term and long-tern gains.

Unfortunately, not all sales lead to gains. Sometimes you have to take a loss. So let's look at how that affects your calculations.

If you have short-term gains *and* losses, net those amounts against each other to arrive at "net short-term gain (or loss)." If you have long-term gains and losses, net those against each other to arrive at "net long-term gain (or loss)." If the combination of both those figures is a gain, you'll enter it on Form 1040. If the combination is a loss, you can use up to $3,000 to offset the rest of your income ($1,500 if married filing separately). If your overall loss is more than $3,000, you'll have to carry the balance forward to future years, where they can offset future gains.

Finally, some sales will be subject to the net investment income tax. This is a new tax of 3.8%, included in the overall Obamacare legislation, on "net investment income," which the law defines to include interest, dividends, capital gains, rents, royalties, and taxable withdrawals from annuities. It kicks in at $200,000 of AGI for individuals and $250,000 for joint filers. So, for example, if you file singly, and you have $210,000 of earned income plus $10,000 of investment income, you'll pay the 3.8% tax on $10,000 of investment income.

Easy peasy, right? So much for the red lights. Now let's start our search for some *green* lights that can help you pay less – or, in some cases, even pay nothing at all, at least for now.

3. Installment Sales

> "If you sell your soul to the Devil, do you need a receipt for tax purposes?"
>
> **Mark Russell**

An installment sale is simply a sale where you receive payment in installments in more than one tax year. This usually involves a series of equal payments over time, such as if you sell a business in three equal installments over a three-year period. However, it also includes balloon payments that you may receive as many as 30 or 40 years down the road. (There's no statutory limit to how long you can wait until you take your cash.)

The main advantage of an installment sale is that it lets you defer tax on your gain until you actually receive those payments. Tax is divided among the actual installments and due as you receive them. Here's the basic concept:

1. Calculate your total gain on the sale.

2. Calculate the percentage of your total sale price consisting of nontaxable basis and the percentage consisting of taxable gain.

3. Multiply each installment by your profit percentage to determine the taxable gain from that installment.

   Example: You buy a building for $600,000 then sell it for $1 million. 40% of your sale price is gain, so 40% of each installment is taxed as capital gain.

Why would you choose an installment sale, rather than taking all your gain up front? Well, in some cases, that's what you have to do to make the sale in the first place. If you're "holding the paper" on the sale, you won't be getting your gains right away . . . so why should you pay tax on them all at once?

The real advantage of the installment sale, though, is avoiding all the nasty consequences of stuffing a big chunk of taxable income into a single year.

   Example: You're married, the kids are out of the house (so there are no dependents), you don't itemize deductions, and you're getting ready to retire. You own a business that grosses $800,000 and nets you $100,000. Assuming there's no other income, you'll be in the 22% tax bracket and your actual bill will be around $6,339.

But what happens when you go to sell that business? Let's say your buyer is willing to pay $800,000 and there's no basis. That means adding $800,000 to your income. That rockets you into the top 20% bracket on capital gains (which otherwise wouldn't kick in until $480,051 of income). It means you'll owe an extra 3.8% in net investment income tax (because your AGI is over $250,000). And it throws you into all sorts of phaseouts that can cost you even more. For example, if you were deducting medical expenses over 7.5% of your income, that threshold jumps from $7,500 to $67,500!

Now let's say you negotiate an installment sale that pays you $100,000 per year for the next eight years. You'll actually pay zero tax on your first $77,400 of gain. (Remember, taxpayers in lower brackets pay zero percent on capital gains.) And structuring the sale in the form of something resembling a "pension" may let you delay drawing Social Security (so you can get higher payments) and delay tapping into your IRAs or other qualified accounts (so you can keep compounding tax-deferred for longer).

The installment sale concept is straightforward enough. Of course, the devil is in the details, and there are all sorts of special rules to complicate things:

- Not all assets qualify for installment sale treatment. Most important, you can't use them for publicly-traded stock, or mutual fund redemptions. (If you have a large enough portfolio, you can always liquidate your interest over time. But that doesn't let you lock in today's price for your shares, and you have to take the chance that prices may fall over that period.)

- You have to charge adequate interest on the unpaid balance. Otherwise, the IRS can recharacterize part of each payment as interest. The minimum rate you have to charge is generally the "applicable federal rate" in effect at the time of the sale. Interest on unpaid installments is taxed as ordinary income, not capital gain.

- If you sell depreciated personal property, like business equipment, you'll have to "recapture" that depreciation and pay tax on it at ordinary income rates. That tax is due immediately in the year of sale; you can't stretch it out the way you can with ordinary capital gains.

- If you sell depreciated real estate, you'll have to recapture that depreciation in the year of sale, too. Tax on that income, also called "unrecaptured Section 1250 gain," is capped at 25%.

- You can't elect installment sale treatment for depreciable property you sell to a business you control or a to trust with you or your spouse as a beneficiary.

- If you sell property with no fixed price, such as an "earnout" sale of a business or property for a fixed percentage of sales or rent, you have to divide the property's basis into the term of the installments, then pay tax on any gain above that amount.

- If your buyer assumes a mortgage, you'll have to subtract that debt from the gross sale price before you calculate your gain on the sale.

- If your buyer unexpectedly prepays any installments, you'll owe tax on the "gain" portion of those installments as you receive them.

- If you elect installment treatment on a sale to a relative (spouse, child, grandchild, parent, grandparent, sibling) and they resell the property within two years of the original sale date, you'll owe tax on the entire remaining unpaid balance the year the relative sells the property.

Here's a special situation that probably won't apply to you – but if it does, it will be one of those "nice problems to have." If the total of installment payments owed to you in any year tops $5 million, you'll owe interest at the federal "underpayment rate" in effect for the last month of the year on the unpaid *income* tax (but not the 3.8% "net investment income tax") on the balance exceeding $5 million.

> **Example**: In 2017, you sell a business for $10 million, payable in 10 installments of $1 million per year starting in 2018. At the end of 2017, what do you owe?
>
> - Start with the $10 million balance.
>
> - Subtract the $5 million threshold, which leaves $5 million subject to the charge (50% of the gain).
>
> - Calculate the tax due on the $10 million. In this case, it will be $2,000,000 (20% of $10 million).
>
> - Multiply the $2,000,000 tax by the 50% subject to the charge (which gives you $1 million).
>
> - Multiply the resulting $1 million by the federal underpayment rate in effect for the last month of the year. (For 2017, that rate was 4%.)
>
> In this case, the interest charge is $40,000. (You'll add that to the regular tax due in the "Other Taxes" section of Form 1040.)

Structured Sales

In some cases, you might want to take advantage of installment sale treatment, but your buyer prefers to pay cash up front. A "structured sale" is a clever way to turn right on red and preserve installment sale treatment for you. Here's how it works:

1. You negotiate a traditional sale with your buyer.

2. Your buyer assigns their obligation to make payments to an independent third-party and pays the purchase price, in cash, to that third party. (Using a third party avoids the "constructive receipt" rules which would otherwise make the sale immediately taxable.)

3. The third party uses the buyer's cash to buy an immediate annuity from a top-rated life insurance company. (An "immediate" annuity is one that begins making payments to you immediately, rather than accumulating income over time.)

4. You pay taxes on your gain as you receive those annuity installments.

Under the regular annuity tax rules, each payment you get will consist of three parts: 1) return of your original basis in whatever asset you sold using the structured sale; 2) capital gains on that sale; and 3) interest income earned in the annuity contract.

Think of a structured sale as exchanging an appreciated asset for a guaranteed income, and you'll be able to quickly decide if it makes sense for your sale. The upside is the way you get to defer the tax on the sale, which means investing more of the proceeds to generate income than if you had simply sold the asset, paid the tax, and been done with it. The downside is the lower rate of return you get from an annuity contract than you might have gotten from an alternative investment. They're generally appropriate for sales between $100,000 and $5 million.

Some advisors have created a similar vehicle where you create a trust and then sell your property to that trust in exchange for the trust's promise to pay you an income over time. Tax on your gain is deferred until you start taking payments from the trust, just as with a traditional installment sale. However, there are two particular problems with this approach. First, it generally involves giving control of post-sale investments to a third-party asset manager, whose fee structure and investment philosophy may or may not meet your overall investment goals. And second, the trust arrangement may not provide sufficient "arms-length" removal from the seller to avoid "constructive receipt" of the sale proceeds, which would make the transaction taxable immediately.

"Installment Sale Coupled with Monetizing Loan"

Here's the biggest downside of most installment sales. You're successfully deferring and minimizing your tax bill. But you don't have your *money*. Oops.

That's fine if you're comfortable exchanging the equity in your asset for an income stream. Plenty of business owners, for example, are happy swapping their business for the equivalent of a pension. They don't *need* it all at one. But that tradeoff may not be the right answer if you want to reinvest your equity from the sale property into something else.

One clever solution involves coupling an installment sale with a monetizing loan to give you cash while still deferring tax on the sale. (Remember, it's not available for publicly-traded securities trading on an active exchange, because those don't qualify for installment sale treatment in the first place). It defers tax on the sale for 30 years while giving you up-front access to nontaxable loan proceeds. It combines tax deferral with a powerful "time value of money" play to essentially shrink the tax bill until it's small enough that you can drown it in a bathtub. Here's how Financial Gravity has helped clients make it work:

1. You negotiate a sale price with your buyer just as you would if you were delighted to get hammered the tax as soon as you close the sale.

2. When it comes time to close, you sell your asset to an unrelated third-party in exchange for a single lump-sum payment due in 30 years.

3. The third party simultaneously sells the asset to the buyer in exchange for your agreed-upon sale price.

So far so good, right? You've sold your asset, and you've used installment sale treatment to defer your tax. Of course, you still don't have your *money*. That's where the monetizing loan comes in.

4. At the same time, you and the third party and the buyer close your original sale, a third-party lender steps in and

extends loan proceeds equal to 93.5% of the sale proceeds to you. (Loan proceeds are nontaxable because they come with the obligation to repay.)

Now you have cash, in an amount nearly equivalent to your pre-tax sale price, and you're free to reinvest it as you see fit.

5. While the loan is outstanding, the third party pays the interest. In fact, the terms of the loan specify the interest is "nonrecourse" to you – the lender cannot come after you for those payments.

6. After 30 years, the whole transaction unwinds. The third party pays you (or your heirs) the purchase price in cash; you use the proceeds to repay the loan, and you pay the tax.

You'll pay tax on your gains at whatever rates are in effect in 30 years. Now, will those rates be lower? Higher? Magic Eight Ball says, "ask again later"!

But the real magic here isn't just the tax deferral. It's the time value of money. That means the real question isn't, "what will the tax rate be on the gains?" The real question will be, "what's the tax bill even *worth* in 30 years, anyway?"

If inflation continues to average just over 2.5%, as it has over the last 30 years, and the rate on long-term capital gains stays at 20%, the tax bill on $1 million of gain in 2019 will be the equivalent of $94,277 in 2049. That's less than half of today's bill, plus 30 years' use of the money in the meantime! If inflation spikes at any time in that 30-year period, as it did in the 1970s, the actual tax will be even less. (Maybe enough to buy a nice self-driving electric car? Maybe one of those personal jet packs, if somebody finally gets around to inventing them?)

Strategies for Your Business

> "I love America, but I can't spend the whole year here. I can't afford the taxes."
>
> **Mick Jagger**

Selling a business usually means selling a collection of business assets such as equipment, goodwill, and the like. Your tax bill depends largely on how you characterize those assets. Smart planning lets you keep more of what you sell. It can even make your business more affordable for your buyer.

If your business is incorporated, you can simply sell your stock. But this is rarely the best choice for buyers, especially when they're acquiring smaller businesses. Buyers can't depreciate stock; they assume liability for corporate claims; and they face double tax selling appreciated assets out of C corporations. This means most small business sales take the form of asset sales.

- Your business name, client list, and goodwill are capital assets. Buyers generally depreciate these over 15 years.

- Covenants not to compete are taxable as ordinary income to sellers. (This suggests you should allocate as *little* of the price as possible to such agreements.)

- Capital equipment (such as cars, trucks, and computers) is taxed as a business property. Your buyer's basis is the sale price of the asset, which he can then depreciate or expense. You'll report recaptured depreciation and capital gain on those assets, depending on their basis and sale price.

- Inventory, supplies, and similar items that you've already expensed are taxed as ordinary income at the time of the sale.

- Continuing service you provide the buyer after the sale is treated as earned income. Since taxes on capital gains are so much lower than taxes on earned income, it makes sense to allocate as little as possible to continued assistance after the sale.

- Real estate included in the sale is taxed like any other investment property. You'll pay tax on "unrecaptured Section 1250 gain" and capital gains; your buyer will depreciate it like any other property.

If you're selling a business, here are two specific strategies you might consider to take advantage of to minimize the tax bill on your exit.

Employee Stock Ownership Plan

Employee stock ownership plans ("ESOPs") are defined contribution retirement plans designed primarily to invest in employer stock. ESOPs qualify for special breaks to encourage employee ownership. They can borrow to buy employer stock; employers can deduct plan contributions above and beyond regular limits to repay plan loans; and employers can generally deduct dividends paid on ESOP stock. But most employers who adopt ESOPs do so to let owners sell stock and postpone tax on the gain. This is a powerful tool for owners who qualify:

- You have to have owned your stock for at least three years before you sell to an ESOP. You can't have acquired it from a qualified plan, exercising stock options, or an employee stock purchase plan.

- The ESOP has to own at least 30% of the corporation after the sale. You can sell up to 50% of the stock and keep control of the business, or you can sell up to 100% to exit completely.

- You have 15 months (beginning three months before the date of sale and ending 12 months after) to reinvest your proceeds in "qualified domestic securities." These are stocks or bonds issued by domestic corporations using at least 50% of their assets in active trade or business and whose passive income for the preceding year does not exceed 25% of gross receipts.

- If you sell those replacement securities during your lifetime, you'll owe tax on your original gains plus any gains you make on those replacement securities. If you're looking for liquidity, rather than mere reinvestment, consider reinvesting your proceeds in special "ESOP notes" which let you borrow up to 90% of their value to draw equity or diversify without selling. These are adjustable-rate notes issued by top-rated borrowers, with terms up to 60 years, and rates pegged to short-term commercial paper.

- Replacement securities enjoy the same stepped-up basis at your death as any other capital asset. This lets you avoid tax on your gains entirely.

- ESOPs aren't cheap to establish or operate. Legal fees and initial business valuations can range from $5,000 up. Annual plan administration and valuation fees add more. This makes ESOPs most appropriate for businesses valued at $1 million or more, with long-term employees you'd like to reward.

Section 1202 Stock

---

§ 1202 "Qualified Small Business Stock"

- Exclude up to 100% of gain up to *greater* of $10 million or 10x basis
- Establish business as as C corp
- Acquire stock at original issue
- ≤ $50 million capitalization
- "Meet active business/industry requirements
- Hold 5+ years

Here's a specific opportunity to use a C corporation to shelter capital gains when you sell. It's called §1202 stock, or "qualified small business stock." And it lets you exclude up to 100% of your gains when you sell, up to the *greater* of $10 million or 10 times your adjusted basis in the stock.

Now that's a heck of a deal. But naturally, not everyone qualifies. So let's take a look at the requirements because they're pretty specific:

- First of all, the company has to have been established as a corporation, taxed as a C corporation, right out the gate. You can't just take some old LLC that's lying on the shelf, file Form 8832 to make an C election, and call it good. You have to establish the entity as a C corp up front.

- You have to acquire your stock directly from the corporation itself, at its original issue. This is for shiny new stock, not dirty used stock.

- Next, the company can't be capitalized at more than $50 million. The goal here is to encourage small businesses, not Exxon spinoffs.

- At least 80% of the value of the business assets have to be used in the active conduct of one or more qualified businesses. This isn't just a wrapper for an investment portfolio.

- Finally, several categories of business are specifically *excluded* from this opportunity. These include:

    - A service business in the fields of health, law, engineering, architecture, accounting, actuarial science, performing arts, consulting, athletics, financial services, or brokerage services

    - A banking, insurance, financing, leasing, investing, or similar business

- A farming business

- A business involving the production of products for which percentage depletion can be claimed

- A business of operating a hotel, motel, restaurant, or similar business

So—lots of technical requirements, and most businesses won't qualify. If you do, however, then you've got a great strategy to exclude a ton of gains when you sell.
This is an especially good strategy for intellectual property.

If your business involves patents, copyrights, or trademarks, consider establishing a Section 1202 corporation and moving those assets into the corporation.

Your exact exclusion depends on when you originally established the corporation:

- If you established it between 8/11/93 and 2/17/09, you can exclude 50% of the gain – however, that amount is also a preference item for alternative minimum tax (AMT).

- If you established it between 2/18/09 and 9/27/10, you can exclude 75%, and it's a preference item.

- Finally, if you established it after 9/27/10, you can exclude 100% of the gain – and there's no AMT consequence.

4. Strategies for Real Estate

> "I shall never use profanity except in discussing house rent and taxes."
>
> **Mark Twain**

Everyone knows that real estate is a great tax shelter. You get to depreciate the cost of your property over 27.5 years for residential property, or 39 years for nonresidential property. And you can depreciate many of the components of your property like land improvements, kitchen appliances, and bathroom fixtures even faster. That means nice tax deductions for a non-cash expenses (although, to be fair, you're not deducting the principal portion of your mortgage payment).

In this case, though, what the tax code giveth, the tax code taketh back. Here's the downside to all those great depreciation deductions. Someday, when you sell, you have to "recapture" them. That means paying back the tax you saved while you depreciated the property *on top of* paying tax on your capital gains! Tax on recaptured depreciation from real estate is capped at 25%, while tax on recaptured personal property included within the real estate is taxed as ordinary income.

In this chapter, we'll cover the rules for avoiding tax on up to $500,000 of gain when you sell your primary residence. Then we'll discuss a long-established strategy that lets you exchange one property for another and "roll" the untaxed gain on the old property into the new property.

Section 121 Exclusion

If you're like most Americans, your home is your single biggest asset. Homeownership is a foundation of "the American Dream," and the tax code offers all sorts of subsidies to encourage homeownership – the mortgage interest deduction, the property tax deduction, and even special credits for energy efficiency.

Real estate also offers you the opportunity to profit from long-term capital gain. If you buy a house and just stay put, odds are good that you'll make a small fortune. Just ask any of the little old ladies who bought 2-bedroom "ramblers" in Silicon Valley in the 1950s! (Actually, scratch that – there aren't any left because they all sold those houses to developers!)

The problem, of course, is that much of that appreciation isn't really "gain." It's really just inflation. Let's say grandma bought her rambler for $50,000 in 1958. Sixty years later, it would take about $438,000 to equal that $50,000. Now, grandma's house may be worth $1 million. But much of that supposed gain is just inflation . . . and why should grandma pay tax on inflation?

And so, the tax code offers a nice tax break that may (or may not) solve that problem when you sell your primary residence. Here's how it works:

The first requirement is that you own the home for two out of the last five years. That's a pretty straightforward test. (If you're married, only one of you has to have owned it.)

The second requirement is that you occupy it as your primary residence for two out of the last five years. This may be a little tougher if you have more than one home. The IRS takes a "facts and circumstances" approach, and looks at where you work, get your mail delivered, vote, and similar factors to make that call.

Those two-year periods don't have to be the same. For example, you could rent the property for two years, buy it, then immediately move out and convert it to a rental property for two more years and still qualify. However, in most cases, the two-year periods will be the same.

The third requirement is that neither you (nor your spouse, if you're married) have used the exclusion within the previous two years.

Next, you'll have to calculate the actual gain on the sale of your property. This may not be as much as you think at first. For example, if you're single, you bought a house in 1999 for $250,000, and plan sell it in 2019 for $600,000, you may think you're on the hook for tax on $100,000 in gain. But if you spent $50,000 to renovate the kitchen and baths in 2008, plus $20,000 to prep it for sale in 2019, plus $36,000 more in commissions to sell it, you'll see that your actual gain is just $244,000.

Once you meet those two-year requirements and determine your gross gain, you can exclude up to $250,000 of gain if you file singly or $500,000 if you file jointly. (Surviving spouses may qualify for the $500,000 exclusion if they sell within two years of the deceased spouse's death. However, stepped-up basis rules may eliminate much of the gain in those situations anyway.)

What happens if you buy a house, expecting to keep it long enough to qualify, and circumstances force you to move? You can pro-rate the $250,000 or $500,000 exclusion over whatever percentage of the two-year requirement you actually meet, if the sale is due to: 1) a change of more than 50 miles in your place of employment; 2) health reasons; or 30 "unforeseen circumstances," which may include death, unemployment, divorce, or even multiple births from the same pregnancy! So, for example, if you get transferred after 12 months of living in your home, you can exclude up to $125,000 or $250,000 of your gain. (And nicely done for buying a place that appreciates so nicely in a year!)

Taxable gains on the sale of your primary residence are also subject to the 3.8% net investment income tax.

In the end, most taxpayers won't ever wind up paying tax on their primary residence. If, however, you're one of them, you might consider the "monetized installment sale" strategy we discussed already, or look into the charitable remainder trust strategy we'll discuss later in this book.

You may even be able to use the exclusion to save tax when you sell vacation or rental property. You do so by moving into the property yourself and occupying it as your primary residence, for the necessary two-year period. You'll have to treat any depreciation you've taken on it if you've used it as rental property as "unrecaptured Section 1250 gain" when you convert rental property to residential use. But, no further tax will be due unless your final gain exceeds that $250,000 or $500,000 exclusion.

Section 1031 Exchanges

"Section 1031" exchanges let you relinquish real estate you hold for trade or business use or for investment, tax-free, for a "like-kind" replacement. (Up until 2018, you could use these exchanges for any kind of business or investment property; however, the Tax Cuts and Jobs Act of 2017 limited the strategy to real estate.)

You can trade up, relocate, diversify, or consolidate properties and defer tax on recaptured depreciation or capital gains until you sell the replacement. You can exchange properties as many times as you like for nearly unlimited tax deferral. Here's how it works:

- "Like-kind" is defined by how you use the property, not its specific character. You can trade raw land for developed acreage, residential property for non-residential property, and even fee-simple ownership for leaseholds of 30 years or longer.

- You'll need a "qualified intermediary" to arrange paperwork and hold sale proceeds to avoid actual receipt, which would trigger immediate tax on your gains. Most title companies and many real estate attorneys offer this service – "exchange accommodators," as they're called, aren't hard to find.

- You need to roll all of the proceeds from your relinquished property into buying your replacement property. The purchase price and any mortgage on the replacement must be equal or greater than that of the original.

- If you receive cash, nonlike-kind property, or mortgage relief (called "boot") in the exchange, the value of that boot is taxable. (You can combine a 1031 exchange with an installment sale to defer tax on boot.)

You don't have to trade one property directly for another. You can relinquish a property, take proceeds in escrow, and roll the proceeds into your replacement. You don't even have to close both properties simultaneously. Consider these possibilities:

"Deferred" exchanges involve selling before you find your replacement. You have up to 45 days from the date you relinquish your original property to identify up to three potential replacements. You have up to 135 days more (or until the due date, including extensions, for filing your return for the year in which you transfer the relinquished property) to actually close on one of those three potential replacements. (Caution: this means that if your sale date is after October 17, you may not get your full 180 days to close on your replacement unless you file an extension for that year's return.)

"Reverse" exchanges let you close on your replacement up to 180 days *before* you relinquish your existing property. You'll need an "accommodation titleholder" (AT) to hold title to the replacement; however, you can guarantee loans for the AT, loan or advance cash to the AT, and rent, lease, or manage the property while held by the AT.

"Improvement" exchanges and "build to suit" exchanges let you sell one property and roll the gain into improving another property that you already own.

Here are a few more considerations for special situations:

- You can use a Section 1031 exchange to transfer real estate to a "related party." These include a spouse, sibling, parent, child, or corporation or partnership you directly or indirectly own more than 50% of. However, that related party has to hold the property at least two years from the time they acquire it from you, or the exchange will be disallowed, and you'll be taxed retroactively on the gain as of the date the related party transfers the property.

- If you convert a replacement property into your principal residence, you'll have to recapture any depreciation you took on the properties as of the date you convert that replacement property to your own personal use. You'll also have to wait at least five years (rather than the typical two) to exclude any gain from your income under the principal residence rules.

- What happens if you buy a property for the long haul, but your plans change? There's no statutory minimum needed to qualify. Many 1031 experts would agree that 24 months is enough; however, sometimes your holding period may be shorter. If a stranger knocks on your door and makes you the proverbial offer that's "too good to be true" on the replacement property you've just acquired, the IRS would apply a facts-and-circumstances test to determine whether you can use another exchange to defer tax on *that* gain.

The 1031 exchange is a staple of tax planning for property owners. It's been around since 1921, making it even older than Betty White. Taxpayers report hundreds of thousands of exchanges each year, deferring tax on billions of dollars in gains. And if you hold the property until your death, you'll escape tax on those gains entirely. However, the 1031 may not be the right solution for several reasons:

- The exchange process itself can be cumbersome. As anyone who has bought real estate knows, dealing with the paperwork and cutting through the red tape is no picnic, especially where banks are concerned. (Pro-tip: if someone's job title includes the word "underwriter," they're not there to make your life easier.)

- It's possible to dot all your i's and cross all your t's and still wind up losing your tax deferral if you can't identify or close on your replacement within those tight 45- and 180-day deadlines.

- When you roll your proceeds into a new property, your depreciation deductions are based in part of the post-depreciation basis you carry over from the relinquished property, rather than the full purchase price of the replacement.

- Tracking basis across multiple properties and multiple exchanges can wreak havoc on even the best accounting systems.

Finally, many sellers don't just want to get rid of a specific property. They want to get out of the headaches of managing real estate entirely. This meant the 1031 exchange offered little relief. However, there are two ways to use the 1031 exchange to stay in real estate without having to manage replacement property:

- In 2002, the IRS established conditions to qualify "tenancy in common" interests (TICs)—shares of larger properties, such as office parks, shopping centers, or apartment complexes—for 1031 exchanges. Essentially, the so-called TIC exchange lets you swap ownership (and, more important, *management*) of your own property for a fractional interest in a property someone *else* manages – along with a regular income payable by the TIC sponsor from the replacement property. This may be attractive if you'd like to retire from active management without giving up section 1031 tax advantages. The key here that makes it all work is that you're getting a fractional interest in the real estate itself – not a share in a partnership or other type of fund that owns the property.

- In 2004, the IRS issued a ruling letting a taxpayer exchange a property for a fractional interest in a "Delaware statutory trust" (DST) that holds a single, larger property or collection of properties. (In this context, "Delaware" just describes the type of trust. The trust itself, and the property in the trust, don't actually have to be in Delaware.) As with the TIC, the DST gives you professional management and eliminates those 3AM phone calls from disgruntled tenants.

The downside to both the 1031 TIC and DST is that your interest won't be as liquid as if you had simply rolled your gain into your own replacement property that you could sell all by yourself. You may be locked into an investment that no longer suits your needs for income, growth, or both.

If the 1031 isn't the answer, you might also consider the "monetized installment sale" strategy we discussed already, or look into the charitable remainder trust strategy we'll discuss later in this book.

5. Charitable Strategies

> "A fine is a tax for doing something wrong. A tax is a fine for doing something right."
>
> **Anonymous**

Everyone knows that charitable contributions are deductible, right? (At least, if you're one of the 10% or so of taxpayers who still itemize.) Charitable giving is a foundation of tax planning. But it's also a foundation of capital gains planning. That's because charitable entities can sell appreciated assets without paying tax on their gains. And that, in turn, lets you transfer appreciated assets into a charitable entity, keep some "strings" to provide yourself an ongoing income, let the charitable entity sell the asset and keep the full pre-tax proceeds to provide that income. In these cases, you're balancing the upside of more income (because you get to reinvest the sale proceeds that otherwise would have gone to taxes) in exchange for the downside of giving up the asset to charity.

There are two primary vehicles for implementing this concept: the charitable remainder trust, in all its various forms, and 2) the pooled income fund.

Charitable Remainder Trust

A charitable remainder trust, or CRT, is usually established to avoid tax on appreciated assets. That's because the trust can do something you *can't* – and that's sell assets without paying tax on the capital gain. So the usual course involves transferring something like a business or appreciated real estate to a trust, letting the trust sell the asset to avoid tax, then paying an income from the trust to you for the remainder of your life. You benefit from reinvesting the full, pre-tax value of the asset to generate more income than if you had paid tax on the sale, and the charity benefits by getting the trust assets at the end of the trust term.

There are two main decisions you'll have to make, and both of these will affect how much you get to deduct. First, how long will the trust last? And second, how do you want to take your income from the trust?

As far as time is concerned, the trust can last for your individual lifetime. It can last for a joint lifetime – typically, you and your spouse. Or it can last for a "period certain" of up to 20 years. The longer the trust lasts, the later the charity gets the principal, which makes for a smaller up-front deduction. This may not be a real issue if your primary goal is to avoid tax on capital gains when selling an appreciated asset, but it's certainly worth considering.

As for the income interest you keep, there are two main flavors. A charitable remainder annuity trust, or "annuitrust," pays a fixed dollar amount every year based on the value of the initial gift. That amount won't grow over time. Let's say you donate a million dollars. If you choose a 5% annuity payment, you'll draw $50,000 from the trust every year. You can choose a payout as low as 5% or as high as 50%

Alternatively, you can choose a "unitrust" that pays a percentage of trust assets every year. This version lets your income grow for inflation if the trust assets grow over time. The minimum payment you can choose is 5%, and there's no statutory maximum.

There are four different flavors of unitrust. A standard unitrust pays the specified percentage of the trust value every year, whether the trust earns that much over time or not. Let's say you donate a million dollars and specify a six percent payout. If the trust's actual income is six percent, you'll take it. If the trust earns just two or three percent – which is actually more likely in today's low interest-rate environment – you'll take the difference out of trust principal.

A "net income" unitrust lets you take out just the net income, whether it meets the specified percentage or not. A "net income makeup charitable remainder unitrust." (Try saying *that* three times fast!) This version lets you use extra income the trust earns today to make up whatever you might have missed in previous years. Let's say you don't need income now, but you want to draw from it in 10 years for retirement. You can invest the trust principal in growth stocks or other assets that don't throw off current income now – then sell those stocks (tax-free) and reinvest in bonds in a decade when you want the income. In essence, you can decide when you want to turn the income spigot on and off.

Finally, the "flip" trust starts out as a "net income" or "net income makeup" CRUT, then "flips" to become a standard trust after a specified triggering event such as passage of time or sale of an unmarketable asset.

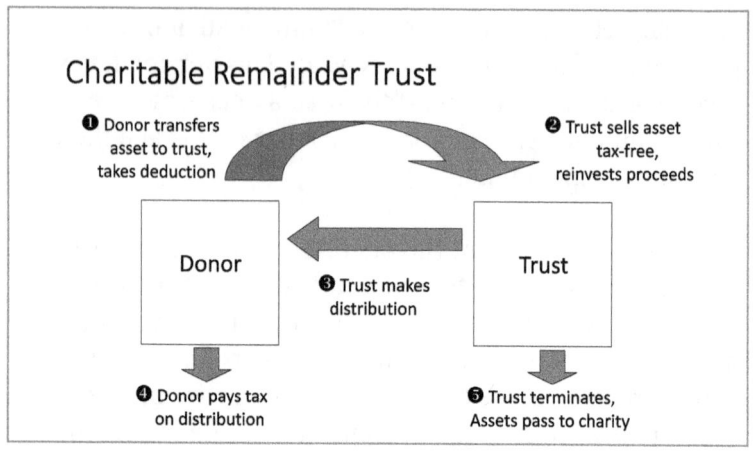

Here's how it works:

1. Once the trust is established (which our partner can help with), you'll transfer the asset to be sold to the trust. At that point, you'll take your deduction for the net present value of the amount expected to go to charity. (More on that below.) Important: there can*not* be a binding contract to sell the asset in place before you transfer it to the trust. (That's why you have to do your *planning* up front!)

2. The trust will then sell the asset to the buyer. This is where the magic happens. Because the trust is a tax-free entity, there's no tax on that capital gain. The trust can reinvest 100% of the asset's sale price, rather than the after-tax amount you would have been left with had you sold in your own name.

3. Over time, the trust will pay you whatever income you specify in the trust documents. This could be an annuity income or whatever flavor of unitrust income you choose. Unitrusts can pay out annually, quarterly, or monthly. Annuitrusts can even pay out weekly if that's what you really, since the dollar amount never changes.

4. The trust files Form 5227 to report income and distributions. The trust itself is nontaxable unless it earns something called "unrelated business taxable income," which usually happens only if the trust is running an actual business or using borrowed money to generate income. You'll pay tax on those distributions according to a delightfully complicated formula.

- Distributions are first taxed as ordinary income, to the extent of the trust's current ordinary income plus any undistributed ordinary income from previous years.

- Next, they're taxed as capital gains to the extent of the trust's current capital gains plus undistributed capital gains from previous years.

- Distributions beyond that are taxed as "other income" exempt from taxes to the extent of the trust's current or undistributed nontaxable income.

- Finally, any distributions beyond those amounts are treated as having been made from principal.

Don't worry, there's not going to be a quiz. I just want you to be aware that the taxes you pay on your CRT income distributions don't necessarily correspond 100% with the trust's actual income.

5. When the trust terminates, after the period certain runs out or the death of the last income beneficiary, the remaining trust assets pass to charity. And now you're all done!

Let's take a look at a case study to see how the strategy can make sense even if you're Ebenezer Scrooge and you have no interest at all in making charitable gifts.

We'll say you have a business for sale. The value is $2 million, and your basis in the business is zero. This is a pretty common scenario, especially for service businesses with no real tangible assets other than items like office furniture and equipment.

If you sell the business outright, you're looking at a hefty tax bill: regular capital gains, net investment income tax, and state income tax. If we assume 20% for regular capital gains, 3.8% for NIIT, plus 5% for state tax, you're looking at $576,000 gone, or nearly 29%. And you're left with just a little over 70% of the gross proceeds to reinvest.

Now let's say you transfer it to a CRT before you sell the business, and structure that trust to pay out the most miserly 10% minimum you can calculate. Now you're looking at zero tax on the sale, and 100% to reinvest. You'll also get a current tax deduction for the 10% gift, even though you don't lose the use of that money that eventually winds up going to charity until your death.

The math is pretty clear. Which would you prefer, a 30% haircut now, or a 10% haircut at your death?

CRUT Deductions

$1 Million Gift, 1.8% Discount Rate		
Donor	Income	Deduction
Single, Age 60	5%	$380,190
Married, Ages 60, 60	5%	$273,450
Married, Ages 70, 60	5%	$324,780
Single, Age 60	6%	$321,200
Married, Ages 60, 60	6%	$213,650
Married, Ages 70, 60	6%	$262,910

Now let's look at how much you actually get to deduct. I'm not going to walk through the math here, because I'm not sure I understand it myself, but the math nerds would explain that your deduction equals the net present value of the expected remainder interest you leave to charity. That, in turn, depends on how much you give, how much income you keep for yourself, how long you'll be taking that income according to the actuarial table, and the "Section 7520 rate" in effect when you make the gift.

As you can see, a single individual age 60 who gives a million dollars, with a discount rate of 1.8%, and keeps a 5% unitrust interest will get a $380,190 deduction. A married couple, both age 60, get a deduction of $273,450. The deduction is lower because two people who are 60 years old have a longer life expectancy than a single 60-year-old, which means the charity has to wait longer to get its money, so the "net present value" of the gift is less.

Finally, a married couple, one age 70 and the other age 60, can deduct $324,780.

Boost the income interest that you keep from 5% to 6%, and the deduction goes slightly down. That's because taking more income for yourself today means less for charity tomorrow.

The main rule you have to watch out for here is this: the net present value of the remainder interest has to be at least 10% of the net fair market value of whatever property you transfer into the trust. That means your maximum deduction can't be more than 90% of the amount you contribute.

Now let's address two concerns that often keep sellers from taking advantage of charitable remainder trusts.

First, if you're concerned about depriving your heirs of the value of your gift, consider establishing a "wealth replacement trust." This is just a trust that you establish to replace the equity that passes to charity at your death.

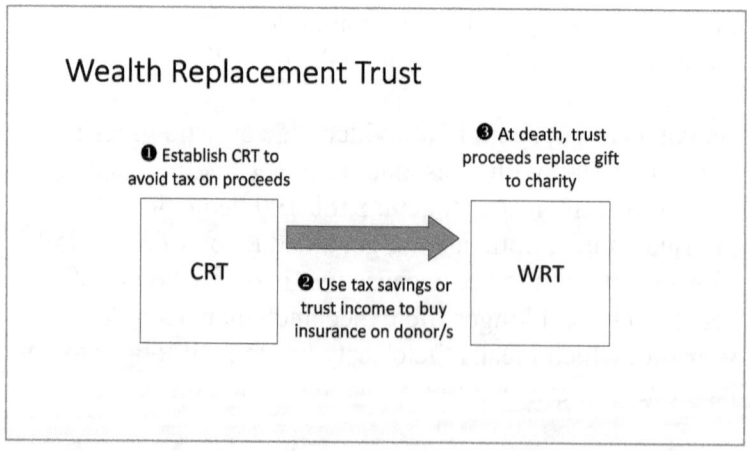

The mechanics are really pretty simple. Once you've established the charitable trust, transferred the appreciated asset to the trust, and sold it, you'll have an income stream from the trust and tax savings from the value of the gift to charity. Simply allocate part of that income or savings to buy insurance on the life of the donor or donors. You can use a single-life policy if the income is payable to a single income beneficiary, or second-to-die coverage if the income is payable for a joint lifetime. If you structure it to qualify as an irrevocable life insurance trust, the proceeds will be income tax-free AND estate tax-free.

This strategy can also address worries you might have about establishing a trust and dying significantly before you collect your expected lifetime payout.

And second, if you're concerned about locking yourself into an income stream that may not always meet your needs – even after looking at flexible "flavors" like the NIMCRUT or flip trust – you should know that a CRT income stream is a capital asset itself that you can sell or restructure. While you can design your trust to give yourself all sorts of options right from the start, there's always a potential escape hatch down the road.

Pooled Income Fund

If you're comfortable with exchanging an asset for an income stream, and you like the idea of contributing to charity, there's another alternative that might not involve quite so much planning and preparation. It's called a pooled income fund, and it's what you'd get if you crossed a charitable remainder fund and a mutual fund.

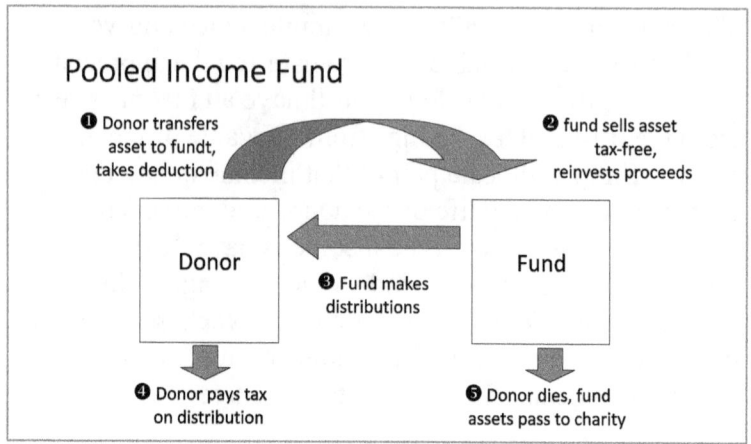

This vehicle lets swap your appreciated asset in exchange for a lifetime income from a share of a diversified portfolio of securities. When the income interest ends, your designated charity gets your share of the assets in that portfolio.

> **Example**: You own a property worth $1 million with a basis of $100,000. If you sell the property, you're looking at federal and state income taxes in the neighborhood of $270,000. Instead, you contribute your property to a pooled income fund with $9 million in assets. The fund sells the property, adds the $1 million to the portfolio, and gives you "participation units" representing your proportional share of the fund's assets.
>
> Your income will be 10% of the fund's income at first, because your $1 million contribution represents 10% of the fair market value of the fund's assets at the time of your contribution (the "determination date.") However, your income percentage will go down over time as the

fund issues new participation units in exchange for new assets.

Here are a few more issues to consider before deciding a pooled income fund is right:

- Most donors choose an income that lasts for their life, or their joint life with their spouse. You can also choose a class of beneficiaries (such as your children) or a consecutive interest (such as yourself, then your children). However, you can't choose a fixed term of years. And naturally, the longer your expected income lasts, the less your charitable deduction will be.

- Some commercial fund sponsors let you choose from among different funds with different investment options. For example, you might choose between a current income fund (designed to produce high current income primarily from fixed-income securities) or a growth and income fund (designed to produce rising income over time by adding equities into the mix). The choice you make may affect the amount you deduct as an up-front charitable gift, as you'll see below.

- Pooled income funds must pay out their income at least annually. However, many pay quarterly or even monthly to make day-to-day budgeting easier.

- Your distributions from the fund will be taxed under the same rules as if you had earned that income directly in your own portfolio. In other words, taxable income interest will be taxed at your regular rate, tax on qualified dividends will be capped as if you had earned them on your own, and tax on long-term capital gains will be taxed just like any other gains you earn.

Distributions are also subject to the net investment income tax for incomes above $200,000 (individual filers) or $250,000 (joint filers).

- If you transfer debt-encumbered property to a pooled income fund, (such as mortgaged real estate), you'll have to pay tax on a fraction of your gain equal to the percentage of the indebtedness. For example, if your property is worth $1 million, your basis is $500,000, and your mortgage is $250,000, you'll owe tax on 25% of your gain (because the $250,000 mortgage balance equals 25% of the property's fair market value).

Now, here's where things get interesting – and where the pooled income fund may really be worth considering. As with a charitable remainder fund, your deduction is based on the discounted present value of the remainder interest we can expect will go to charity. Ordinarily, you'll calculate this based on three factors:

1. The birthdate of the income beneficiary or beneficiaries,

2. The fair market value of the asset/s you transfer into the fund, and

3. The fund's highest rate of return during the preceding three years.

However, if the fund you choose has existed for fewer than three years, you can substitute an assumed rate of return for that third factor above. You'll start by taking the average annual Applicable Federal Midterm Rate (as described in IRC §7520 and rounded to the nearest 2/10ths) for each of the three taxable years preceding the year of the transfer. Then you'll *subtract* one percent to arrive at your final rate.

With interest rates as low as they currently are, this may let you claim significantly higher deductions for contributions to a new pooled income fund than you might otherwise claim for contributions to a "seasoned" fund or a charitable remainder trust. In fact, some pooled income fund sponsors open new funds periodically to take specific advantage of this opportunity.

Contributions to pooled income funds are treated as gifts to public charities. This means you can deduct up to 50% of your AGI and carry any excess forward for up to five years.

6. Strategies for Your Portfolio

> "Buy a stock, if it goes up, sell it, if it goes down, don't buy it."
>
> **Yogi Berra**

Successful investing isn't always easy, especially if you don't have a discipline like Financial Gravity's Factor-Based Investing® to guide you. But it's even harder when you realize you have to beat the IRS, too.

Paying tax on plain vanilla stocks and bonds is pretty simple. (Buy low, sell high, pay tax on the difference.) The real challenge comes when you step up to packaged investment products like mutual funds, exchange-traded funds, and similar vehicles. So, let's take a look at how those structures help shape your ultimate tax consequences – and what you can do about it.

Strategies for Mutual Funds

Mutual funds can help you diversify an investment in cases where you can't afford a portfolio of individual securities. However, their structure creates several tax inefficiencies that can weigh down performance in taxable accounts, especially as they compound over time:

- Income dividends consist of income earned by the fund's portfolio — bond interest, stock dividends, etc. These are taxable immediately, even when you choose to reinvest them back into the fund.

- Capital gains dividends are profits from sale of fund assets. These are generally taxed as long-term capital gains, regardless of how long you've owned your shares. These are also taxable immediately, even when you reinvest them back into the fund.

- Capital gains dividends can even wind up forcing you to pay tax on gains that accumulate *before* you buy into the fund.

    Example: On January 1, The XYZ Growth Fund buys Microsplat at $40 per share. On July 1, you invest in the fund when Microsplat trades at $60 per share. On December 1, the fund sells Microsplat at $80. You'll get a capital gains distribution and owe tax on your share of the full Microsplat gain, even though you personally benefit from just half of it.

- At this point, you're probably thinking that paying tax on someone *else's* capital gains is the worst thing that can happen in a mutual fund. Sadly, you would be wrong. Here's the real killer problem for mutual funds in taxable accounts. Capital gains dividends can even force you to pay tax on *losing* positions.

    Example: On January 1, the XYZ Growth Fund buys Microsplat at $40 per share. On July 1, you invest in the fund with Microsplat trades at $80 per share. On

December 1, the fund sells Microsplat at $60. You'll get a capital gains distribution and owe tax on your share of the fund's $20 gain, even though your piece of the fund actually *lost* that much.

So, while funds offer you the chance to pool your capital with other shareholders, they can force you pay tax based on other shareholders' buying and selling decisions. Keep this trade-off in mind before you invest.

Here are some strategies to minimize tax bills from capital gains distributions:

1. Consider index funds to passively track indexes such as the S&P 500 or Russell 2000. These funds avoid the frequent sales that rack up taxes with actively managed funds. That's because they sell only when they need to redeem shares or the underlying index itself changes.

2. Consider exchange-traded funds ("ETFs"), closed-end index funds that trade on an established exchange. They offer similar advantages as open-ended index funds. And they trade just like stocks, which lets you buy and sell throughout the day, use stop orders and limit orders, and short sales. (Downside: you'll probably pay some sort of commission to trade ETFs, and you can't automatically reinvest shares like with open-end funds.)

3. Consider tax-managed funds, which focus on after-tax returns by avoiding turnover, harvesting tax losses, and selling specific shares to minimize taxable gains. Some also impose early-redemption fees to discourage withdrawals that might force managers to sell shares and realize gains.

4. Look for funds with high "return after taxes." This figure, calculated by Morningstar Mutual Funds, reports each fund's annualized after-tax return. Morningstar calculates this figure twice, once for "return after taxes on distributions" and again for "return after taxes on distributions and sales."

5. Look for funds with low "tax cost ratios." This Morningstar figure represents the percentage-point reduction in an annualized return that you lose to income taxes.

6. Look for funds with low "Potential Capital Gains Exposure." This Morningstar figure reports what percentage of a fund's total assets represents undistributed capital appreciation. If the fund were liquidated today, this embedded capital gain would be taxable to shareholders. Embedded capital gains can be real ticking tax time bombs. In fact, some funds have deliberately distributed capital gains to existing shareholders in order to cut embedded gains to attract new shareholders!

7. Avoid funds with high turnover. This isn't a perfect measure of tax efficiency, but it's a useful indicator once you've narrowed your fund choices down to a few finalists.

Finally, consider separately managed accounts ("SMAs"). These are managed money alternatives that give you the tax advantages of holding individual securities rather than a piece of a fund. Investing in mutual funds means choosing a manager, then paying cash for a piece of the fund itself. Your manager directs the fund, which owns the underlying investments. SMAs, in contrast, means choosing a manager, then give them cash or securities to open a separate account of your own. Your manager directs your portfolio, just like with a mutual fund. But with SMAs, you own the underlying securities yourself. – even if it means owning a fraction of a share rather than a round share amount.

This subtle difference offers important tax and investment advantages:

- SMAs let your manager invest specifically for taxable accounts. You can choose accounts that avoid turnover, match gains and losses, and sell high-basis stock first. You can direct your manager to realize gains or losses to manage your tax liability. Most mutual funds, in contrast,
- accept both taxable and tax-deferred money and manage solely for pretax returns.

- SMAs can serve as "completion funds" to round out large holdings in a single company or industry. If you've retired from Boeing, Microsoft, or P&G with a big block of their stock, the last thing you need is more P&G. SMAs let you avoid your former employer, or your employer's entire market segment (tech, consumer goods, etc.), while exposing you to technology, finance, utilities, and other sectors.

- SMAs don't carry embedded capital gains like funds. SMAs establish separate cost bases and holding periods for each security you buy, insulating you from other shareholders.

- SMAs let you carve out specific securities from your portfolio to give to someone else in your family or to your favorite charity.

- Many SMAs will open an account with securities you already own. This saves you from liquidating holdings and paying immediate tax in order to participate.

- If your manager stinks, you can move your account to another without liquidating holdings and recognizing gains. With mutual funds, in contrast, you have to sell your shares and pay your taxes in order to move to a new fund. (Of course, if you're moving because your manager stinks, you'll probably *want* to liquidate at least some of their picks! The point is, investing through SMAs lets you do it on your own schedule, rather than all at once.)

There are three ways to hire SMA managers. You can find and hire them yourself. You can engage an independent consultant to find and monitor them. Or you can open a "wrap account" for a bundle of services including asset allocation, investment management, performance reporting, commissions, and fees. Wrap programs can include dozens of styles and managers, and open doors you might not otherwise be able to afford.

It used to be that fees for separately managed accounts were generally higher than fees for mutual funds. But today's SMA managers are harnessing technologies that drive down the cost of tracking and managing individual securities. This means that investing in SMAs can actually cost less than investing in retail funds!

Tax Loss Harvesting

Harvesting tax losses ("tax swaps") involves selling one asset at a loss then buying a similar but not "substantially identical" replacement. The swap leaves your portfolio looking the same — but lets you claim a deduction for the loss on your original asset. You can use swaps with individual stocks, bonds, and mutual funds. For example, you can swap one municipal bond for another, one computer manufacturer for another, or one growth fund for another. You can use short- and long-term losses to offset unlimited gains, and you can deduct up to $3,000 in capital losses against ordinary income ($1,500 for married couples filing separately.)

> **Example**: On January 3, you buy 100 shares of Starsky Growth Fund at $100 each. On June 30, those shares are worth $80 each. You sell to realize $2,000 in taxable loss, then reinvest the $8,000 proceeds in the Hutch Growth Fund.

Tax loss harvesting is a very basic strategy. But implementing it can be psychologically hard. Most investors are reluctant to sell their losing positions because it essentially means admitting a mistake – they made a poor choice to buy in the first place. But recent research suggests that tax loss harvesting boosts after-tax returns significantly. This suggests that regular tax-loss harvesting should be a part of every taxable investor's plan.

Here are some limits to beware:

- If you, your spouse, or a corporation you control replaces the original investment with a substantially identical security (or a contract or option to acquire a substantially identical security) within 30 days before or after your sale, your loss is disallowed as a wash sale

- If you just can't bear to give up your stake in a specific stock – but you still want to realize a loss – consider "doubling up," or buying an identical lot more than 31 days before selling your old lot.

- It's not clear how similar two mutual funds can appear before becoming "substantially identical." It would be aggressive to swap one fund family's S&P 500 index fund for another family's same offering. However, it shouldn't be a problem swapping an S&P 500 fund for, say, a Russell 1000 fund.

- The IRS doesn't explicitly prohibit you from using an IRA, qualified plan, or trust to avoid the wash sale rule by selling a holding from a taxable account, replacing it in the IRA, qualified plan, or trust, then claiming the loss in the taxable account. However, the "related party" rules suggest that this would be an aggressive strategy.

If you use separate accounts to manage your money, make sure your managers communicate. Otherwise, one manager's buys could jeopardize tax losses from another manager' sales.

Tax-Engineered Products

"Tax-engineered products" are a set of strategies that let you protect your stock gains and monetize stocks (convert them into cash), while deferring or eliminating taxes you'd pay to sell them outright. These advanced strategies are available for substantial six- and seven-figure gains:

- Stock loan programs use custom derivatives to let you borrow against your stock. These are similar to traditional margin loans, but generally let you borrow up to 90% of your equity (as opposed to the traditional 50% for margin loans).

- Collars use special put and call options to hedge your stock position so that you can borrow more against it. First, sell a "call" option requiring you to sell the stock at a certain price. Then use the proceeds from that call to buy a "put" option letting you sell if the stock falls below a certain price and protecting you from a fall in the price. The bank writing the contracts uses "over-the-counter" options, exercisable under "European" rules only at the expiration of the option. With the stock safely "collared" (meaning, essentially that you won't lose money if the share prices trades below the put price), you can borrow up to 90% of the position's value. You can choose a zero-cost collar, where the sale of the call generates just enough to buy the put. Or you can choose an income-producing collar to help pay the interest on the loan. While the collar is in place, you'll retain voting rights and keep some, but not necessarily all of your dividends. Your ultimate gain or loss at the collar's expiration depends on the stock's price at that time.

- Variable prepaid forwards are agreements to sell shares at a future date in exchange for a specified payment today. The investment bank writing the contract specifies a minimum "floor price" and maximum "cap price," writes options to hedge its risk, then prepays you a specified amount (typically equal to 75-90% of your stock's current value). When the position expires, you'll deliver as much stock as it takes to fulfill your obligation, depending on its price at that time. If the price doubles, for example, you'll deliver just half of your shares to satisfy your obligation. Or you can renew the arrangement to defer the tax even further.

- Swap funds let you exchange your low-basis stock or other assets into a partnership made up of other investors. There's no tax due on the exchange, and the net result is that you wind up owning shares in a more diversified portfolio consisting of all the investors' partnership contributions. (The partnership itself can sell those assets to further diversify its portfolio.) Your main concern is to make sure the fund gives you the diversification you need. If you're a dot-com millionaire, a fund full of other dot-com stocks isn't likely to give you the diversification you want.

8. After-Sale Offsets

> "There is no such thing as a good tax."
>
> **Winston Churchill**

Uh oh. You bought low and sold high, just like you were supposed to do. But you didn't do any *planning* to pay less on the difference. (You should have picked up this book earlier!) Or maybe none of the other strategies we've discussed were a fit. Now you're stuck with a big tax bill, and there's nothing you can do about it.

Or is there . . . ?

What if there was a "tax time machine" you could use to go back in time to before you sold your asset, recognized your gains, and triggered your obligation to pay tax? Well, there's not. (Sorry.) But here are two final strategies you might consider using to offset capital gains you've already realized. Both of them are based on the principle of finding deductions to take in the year of sale to offset the taxable income from the sale.

Charitable Gifts

If you're already charitably inclined, you can use charitable gifts to create deductions to offset the tax on your gains.

I could write an entire book on charitable giving strategies. In fact, that's the topic of the next book in this series! But it's worth pointing out some charitable strategies that you might consider after a sale, even if you miss out on tools like the charitable remainder trust or pooled income fund:

Straight charitable gifts reduce your taxable income by one dollar for every dollar you give. Essentially, giving away your gain, even after the fact, can avoid the tax you would otherwise owe on that gain. Of course, giving away the gain means you won't have it to spend.

A donor-advised fund is a vehicle administered by a public charity that lets you make and deduct a gift now, while reserving the right to designate the beneficiary later. Your gifts grow tax-free under the fund's umbrella. A donor-advised fund also lets you bunch several years' worth of ordinary deductions into a single high-income year, without having to actually donate it to the end recipient.

If you're like many people, you make consistent gifts to, say, your church, year after year after year. A donor-advised fund lets you stockpile your deductions for those gifts now, when the tax bite on your income is unusually high from an extraordinary capital gain.

> **Example**: Your regular salary is $100,000 per year and you tithe $10,000 per year of that to your church. In 2019, you sell a plot of land you inherited years ago from your parents for a $100,000 gain. A donor-advised

fund would let you contribute $100,000 now and pay it out at $10,000 per year from the fund rather than your own pocket. This lets you "take home" an extra $10,000 per year (minus the tax on that income), essentially spreading out the tax on your $100,000 gain over the next 10 years.

Finally, if you have $250,000 or more to give, a charitable *lead* trust, or CLT (as opposed to the charitable *remainder* trust we discussed in Chapter Six) lets you set aside a pool of money to provide an income stream for a certain period of time, then get the whole pool back at the end of the period. In that sense, it's like a donor-advised fund in that it lets you accelerate deductions for years' worth of gifts into a single year.

A CLT splits the trust assets into two pieces:

1. First, there's an income interest payable to charity for a fixed period of years or the life of one or more individuals. As with the charitable remainder trust, this can be a fixed dollar amount (an "annuitrust") or percentage of assets (a "unitrust"). It can also grow over time in a series of steps or with a balloon payment at the end.

2. When the income interest ends, the trust assets revert back to you or another noncharitable beneficiary.

A "grantor" CLT lets you deduct the full net present value of the interest you donate to charity in the year you establish the trust. This value is based on several factors, including the IRS "Section 7520 rate" in effect for the month you make the gift, the dollar amount or unitrust percentage of income you reserve for the charity, and the period of time the charitable income lasts.

> **Example**: You establish a CLT with $1 million when the discount rate is 1.4%. If you give the charity a 5% annuitrust income interest for 20 years and keep the remainder interest for yourself, your deduction will be $636,271. If you bump the annuitrust up to 5.77%, you can deduct the full $1 million you transfer into trust.

Here's the magic in the strategy. Remember, at the end of the trust term you (or your heirs) will be getting back the principal. The value of that remainder interest is calculated using the Section 7520 rate in effect for the month you make the gift. But if the trust assets outperform that rate, *you* get to keep the difference! For December 2018, that rate was 3.6%. If you think you can do better than 3.6% over the trust term – typically 10-20 years, if not a lifetime – then the CLT tax advantages can actually outweigh the cost of the charitable giving!

Now here's the downside to the whole arrangement – but it's hardly insurmountable. Income the grantor CLT earns will be taxable back to you. This makes it imperative to invest trust assets in a tax-efficient manner to minimize tax on so-called "phantom income."

You can fund a CLT with cash, securities, real estate, or any combination of assets. This makes it appropriate for "catch-up planning" after you've sold something without doing your planning homework first because you can use part of the proceeds from that gain to fund the strategy.

Oil & Gas

Oil and gas investments have always enjoyed rich tax advantages designed to encourage drilling and energy production. Way back in 1934, FDR's Treasury Secretary Henry Morgenthau recommended eliminating some of the percentage depletion allowance, but later reported that "nothing was done, presumably because of the heavy pressure from the large oil and mining companies which are profiting immensely from them." (Sound familiar?) If oil and gas make sense as part of your overall portfolio, these programs let you take advantage of four specific tax breaks:

1. You can deduct your share of intangible drilling and development costs ("IDC") like labor, fuel, supplies, and other expenses the sponsor incurs in launching the program. These up-front expenses are deductible immediately when you invest, even if there's no current income to offset. Generally, program sponsors will borrow to increase the program's overall investment. This leverage may mean that nearly all of your initial investment is deductible in the year you invest.

2. You can depreciate your share of the equipment used to extract resources from the ground. Oil and gas are capital-heavy industries, and the industry has lobbied hard for faster write-offs, so these deductions can be quite valuable.

3. You can deduct your share of any interest the sponsor pays to finance the program. Most of these activities are highly leveraged, so this means high interest deductions.

4. You can deduct a percentage of your income from the program each year as a "depletion allowance" to reflect the economic reality that someday the well will run dry. This rule takes advantage of the same principle as depreciation deductions for real estate or business equipment. Typically, this equals 15% of your income from the program.

These are all valuable tax breaks. But it's the first one that plays the biggest part in using oil & gas programs to offset capital gains.

Let's say you paid $10,000 for a slug of Apple stock, then sold it years later for $50,000. That's a pretty nice gain! But it's a publicly-traded stock, so you couldn't use an installment sale. The gain wasn't enough to justify a charitable remainder trust. And the value of your position wasn't enough for any of the tax-engineered products we discussed. So now you're stuck with $40,000 in gain.

If you turn around and invest the $50,000 of proceeds in a typical oil & gas program, you may be able to deduct 80-95% of that amount as soon as you invest. That should be enough, all by itself, to eliminate the actual tax on your gain.

Of course, the real question, as with any investment, is whether it makes sense in your portfolio. Remember, the goal usually isn't just to avoid tax – it's to earn the highest after-tax rate of return consistent with your risk tolerance and other goals.

9. Qualified Opportunity Zones

> "The wages of sin are death, but by the time taxes are taken out, it's just sort of a tired feeling."
> **Paula Poundstone**

The Tax Cuts and Jobs Act focused most of its attention on flattening corporate tax rates, creating a new category of "qualified business income," and lowering personal rates. But the 2017 legislation also introduced a new capital gains mitigation strategy in the form of Qualified Opportunity Zones (QOZs). The goal of this provision is to encourage investing in specific "economically distressed" communities.

This sort of targeting has been a longtime goal of many legislators. Representative Jack Kemp, who helped champion the 1986 tax reform, promoted the concept of "opportunity zones" throughout his career, and would be delighted to see them finally brought to life. Washington has previously authorized tax breaks for so-called "Empowerment Zones" and "Renewal Communities." But the 2017 program is far more expansive than previous efforts. The IRS has designated 8,700 QOZs, or about 12% of the country's census tracts. Previous programs, in contrast, authorized just 40 empowerment zones and 40 renewal communities for the entire country.

The TCJA accomplishes the goal of promoting investment in opportunity zones in two ways: First, it lets you postpone tax on gains in any investment if you roll the proceeds into an approved Qualified Opportunity Fund (QOF). And second, you can exclude part or all of the gains you earn in the QOF itself if you hold the position long enough.

Tax Deferral

The first part of the legislation involves deferring tax on existing gains.

1. You can defer tax on any appreciated property you currently have to sell. This can include real estate, business interests, publicly-traded securities, and mutual fund shares.

2. You have to sell the property to an unrelated party. You can't sell it from yourself to your own corporation, for example, to raise your basis in the property.

3. You have 180 days from the date you sell your appreciated property to roll your proceeds into the qualified opportunity fund.

4. At this writing, we don't yet know exactly you'll report these transactions. The IRS has stated that you'll make the election on the return for the year when you would have reported the gains if you hadn't chosen to defer them.

5. You don't have to roll the entire proceeds of the sale into the QOF. You can pocket your tax-free basis in your original investment and roll just the gain into the fund.

Of course, all good things someday come to an end – even tax deferral. Your original gain that you roll into the QOF becomes taxable when you sell the QOF or on December 31, 2026, whichever comes first. On that date, even if you haven't sold your QOF, your gain on your original property becomes taxable, and you'll need to be ready to pay the tax on your original gain with funds from another source.

Qualified opportunity zones expire completely on December 31, 2028. You'll still be able to hold funds you've invested in before that date – you just won't be able to make any new investments. (Of course, Washington can always choose to extend that deadline in future legislation.)

Qualified Opportunity Fund

So, what exactly constitutes a qualified opportunity zone? The legislation authorized each state, plus the District of Columbia and U.S. possessions, to nominate census tracts where the median family income is under 80% of the statewide figure *or* where the poverty rate is at least 20% to participate in the program. The IRS published the final list on July 9, 2018 (which is why you may not have heard much about the program until now). You'll find it in IRS Notice 2018-48.

These zones aren't necessarily as blighted as you may think. For example, in November 2018, Amazon announced plans to establish a second headquarters in the

Long Island City neighborhood of New York. The area is gentrifying fast, with gleaming new high-rise condos and apartments with stunning Manhattan views, and a median household income of $138,000. It's also – you guessed it – a qualified opportunity zone.

Now that we understand qualified opportunity *zones*, what are qualified opportunity *funds*? Those are simply corporations or partnerships created for the purpose of investing in a QOZ and holding at least 90% of their assets in "QOZ property." QOZ property, in turn, is tangible property, including real estate, acquired after December 31, 2017, which is first used within the zone by the fund, or which is "substantially improved" by the fund after acquisition. To substantially improve the property, the fund must increase the property's basis by more than 100% within a 30-month period after the acquisition.

So, take your appreciated property, sell it, and roll part of the gain into a QOF to defer taxes. Are there any more advantages? Yes:

1. If you hold your investment in a QOF for five years, you can increase your basis in the QOF by 10% of the deferred gain.

2. If you hold your investment in a QOF for seven years, you can increase your basis in the QOF by 15% of the deferred gain.

3. Finally, if you hold your investment in the QOF for 10 years, you can increase your basis in the QOF to the fund's fair market value as of the date you sell or exchange it.

Ok, let's break that down into plain English. Let's say you bought stock in Microsplat for $100,000. Now it's worth $1,000,000, and you'd like to sell. But you don't relish the thought of paying six figures in tax on that gain. (You could buy a couple of Teslas with all that money!) So, you roll your $900,000 gain into a QOF on January 1, 2019. Your basis in the QOF, at that point, is zero, because it consists of untaxed Microsplat gain.

On January 1, 2024, you can increase your basis in that $900,000 QOF investment by $90,000, or 10% of the $900,000 gain you deferred when you sold the Microsplat. If you sell at that point, you'll owe tax on the remaining $810,000 of Microsplat gain, plus any appreciation in the QOF above the original $900,000 investment.

On January 1, 2026, you can increase your basis in your $900,000 QOF investment by another $45,000, bringing the total increase to 15% of the $900,000 gain you deferred when you sold the Microsplat. If you sell at that point, you'll owe tax on the remaining $765,000 of Microsplat gain, plus any appreciation in the QOF above the original $900,000 investment.

On December 31, 2026, you'll owe tax on $765,000 of the Microsplat gain ($900,000 minus the $135,000 step-up in basis) whether you've sold your QOF or not. The good news is, at that point you'll increase your basis in the QOF by the amount of gain you pay tax on. So your basis in the QOF will now equal your original $900,000 Microsplat gain, even though you've paid tax on just $765,000 of it. If you sell your QOF, you'll owe tax on any proceeds above your new $900,000 basis.

Finally, on January 1, 2029, you'll meet the 10-year holding period. That means if you sell your QOF interest for, say, for $1.9 million your basis will step up to that full $1.9 million amount. That, in turn, means you'll pay *no* tax on the $1 million gain on the QOF itself.

Easy, right? (Right!)

Your chances to claim the 10% and 15% basis step-ups expire on January 1, 2027. That means, if you want to take advantage of the 10% basis step-up, you have to invest in the QOF by December 31, 2021 (in order to meet the five-year holding period requirement by December 21, 2026). If you want to take advantage of the 15% basis step-up, you have to invest in the QOF by December 31, 2019 (in order to meet the seven-year holding period requirement by December 31, 2026).

Where do you *find* these qualified opportunity funds? You can Google them and you'll find no shortage of managers clamoring for your investment dollars. You can find one through our Financial Gravity partner network. You can even start your own fund, even if you're the only investor. There's no requirement that you have to pool funds with unrelated investors.

The tax advantages with QOZs and QOFs seem like an obvious draw. Who wouldn't love a strategy that lets them defer tax on one investment and possibly avoid it on the replacement? But in the end, choosing to deploy assets in a QOF should be an investment decision. Is QOF investing really right for you? That really turns on how the fund you choose, and the assets it buys, fit within your overall portfolio.

The new law's tax breaks will probably create a ton of demand for QOZ investments, and that alone should help boost returns. But will a QOF give you the liquidity or income you need from the proceeds of your original investment? If not, then don't let the tax tail wag the investment dog. Remember, your real goal isn't just to avoid taxes. (You can accomplish *that* just by not making any money!) Your real goal should be to make the right investment decision for your needs and circumstances – *then* find the most tax-efficient way to make it.

Here's a second factor to consider, and this is one we have to look at with any tax deferral strategy. We know what the tax rules look like today. But we don't know what they'll look like on December 31, 2026, when tax on deferred gain is due. It's at least plausible that rates will go up between now and then – in which case paying later actually means paying more.

There's one final technical but important *dis*advantage buried in the QOF fine print that you'll need to consider before diving in. If you die while you own an investment in a QOF, any untaxed gain on the investment you deferred into that fund is considered "income in respect of a decedent," which is legalese for "income we didn't tax you on while you were alive so we're going to tax you on it now that you're dead." There's no chance to benefit from the usual stepped-up basis that you would have enjoyed if you had just held your original investment, or an after-tax replacement, until you died. So, before you commit to a QOF, you might want to ask yourself just how well you're feeling, and whether you think you'll be around longer than your QOF. (Are you taking your vitamins? Eating all your kale?)

Questions and Notes

Questions and Notes